Date: 5/27/16

**J 599.352 GRE
Gregory, Josh,
Rats /**

RATS

by Josh Gregory

Children's Press®

An Imprint of Scholastic Inc.

Content Consultant
Dr. Stephen S. Ditchkoff
Professor of Wildlife Ecology and Management
Auburn University
Auburn, Alabama

Photographs ©: cover: Oleg Kozlov/Alamy Images; 1: blickwinkel/
Alamy Images; 2, 3: Pat Tuson/Alamy Images; 2, 3 main: Pam7/
Dreamstime; 4, 5 background: Anni Sommer/Superstock, Inc.; 5
top, 5 bottom: Tom McHugh/Science Source; 6: Don Mammoser/
Shutterstock, Inc.; 7: Don Mammoser/Shutterstock, Inc.; 8, 9: Pat
Tuson/Alamy Images; 10, 11: Minden Pictures/Superstock, Inc.; 12,
13: Ben Queenborough/Media Bakery; 14, 15: Derek Middleton/
Minden Pictures; 16, 17: blickwinkel/Alamy Images; 18, 19: Fer
Gregory/Shutterstock, Inc.; 20, 21: Lenartowski/Superstock, Inc.;
22, 23: Minden Pictures/Superstock, Inc.; 24, 25: Anni Sommer/
Superstock, Inc.; 26, 27: Tom McHugh/Science Source; 28, 29:
NHPA/Superstock, Inc.; 30, 31: imageBROKER/Alamy Images;
32, 33: Tom McHugh/Science Source; 34, 35: GIRAL/Superstock,
Inc.; 36, 37: Cusp/Superstock, Inc.; 38, 39: Charanya Phaengsri/
Shutterstock, Inc.; 40, 41: roger parkes/Alamy Images; 44, 45
background: Pam7/Dreamstime; 46: blickwinkel/Alamy Images.

Library of Congress Cataloging-in-Publication Data
Gregory, Josh, author.
  Rats / by Josh Gregory.
    pages cm. — (Nature's children)
  Summary: "The book details the life and habits of rats."— Provided by
publisher.
  Includes bibliographical references and index.
  ISBN 978-0-531-22723-7 (library binding) — ISBN 978-0-531-
22521-9 (pbk.)
  1. Rattus norvegicus—Juvenile literature. 2. Rats—Juvenile literature. I.
Title. II. Series: Nature's children (New York, N.Y.)
  QL737.R666G74 2016
  599.35'2—dc23   2015021723

Printed in China 62
SCHOLASTIC, CHILDREN'S PRESS, and associated logos are
trademarks and/or registered trademarks of Scholastic Inc.

1 2 3 4 5 6 7 8 9 10 R 25 24 23 22 21 20 19 18 17 16

Rats

Class	Mammalia
Order	Rodentia
Family	Muridae
Genus	*Rattus*
Species	56 species
World distribution	Every continent except Antarctica
Habitat	Forests, fields, urban areas
Distinctive physical characteristics	Body measuring 6.7 to 8.3 inches (17 to 21 centimeters) long; narrow tail that is usually about the same length as the body; pointy face; large ears and eyes; fur in shades of brown, black, white, and gray
Habits	Most species are nocturnal; live in burrows or other hidden spaces; able to reproduce very rapidly; possess a strong ability to learn new things; tend to live together in large groups; communicate using sound, scent, and body language; able to adapt to human environments
Diet	Varies from species to species; usually omnivorous, with some species preferring live prey and others preferring plants

RATS

Contents

6 CHAPTER 1
Rats in the City

14 CHAPTER 2
Survival Skills

25 CHAPTER 3
Strength in Numbers

30 CHAPTER 4
Rodent Relatives

34 CHAPTER 5
Living with Rats

42 Words to Know
44 Habitat Map
46 Find Out More
47 Index
48 About the Author

Rats in the City

As you walk down the busy city sidewalk, you are amazed at the amount of activity around you. Crowds of people make their way to and from shops and restaurants. You hear bits and pieces of different songs coming from businesses and car stereos. There are bright lights everywhere.

All of a sudden, a small, furry animal darts past your feet. Is it someone's escaped pet? You look closely as the animal runs into a nearby alley. It's too small to be a dog or a cat. You also notice its long, hairless tail. It's a rat!

A busy city may be one of the last places you'd expect to find a wild animal searching for food. However, rats are just as likely to live in the basement of an old building as they are to live in a forest or some other wild **habitat**. These clever animals are found almost everywhere people live.

Some rats thrive in human communities.

Small and Furry

There are many different **species** of rats. While each has a slightly different appearance, all rats share the same basic characteristics. These small creatures have long, furry bodies and very narrow tails. Their faces are pointed, and they have large eyes and ears. Fur color varies between species. Most rats are different combinations of gray, brown, white, and black.

The average rat's body is around 6.7 to 8.3 inches (17 to 21 centimeters) long. Some species are slightly larger or smaller. Most species' tails are about the same length as their body, but that can vary as well. One of the largest species is the Sulawesian white-tailed rat. It can grow to be 7.5 to 10.6 inches (19 to 27 cm) long with a tail that is slightly longer than its body. One of the smallest is the Osgood's rat. Its body is around 4.7 to 6.7 inches (12 to 17 cm) long. Its tail is a little shorter than its body.

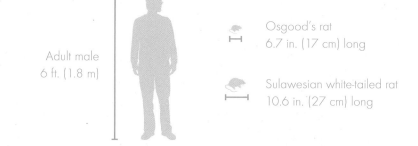

Adult male
6 ft. (1.8 m)

Osgood's rat
6.7 in. (17 cm) long

Sulawesian white-tailed rat
10.6 in. (27 cm) long

Many rats have several different colors of fur.

Rats Everywhere

Rats live in many different habitats. Some are found only in wild areas, while others are more common in **urban** locations. Most wild rat species are native to Asia, Australia, or New Guinea. They often live in forests, fields, and other outdoor areas.

Two of the most common rat species are the brown rat (also known as the Norway rat) and the house rat (also called the black rat). The brown rat was once native to northern China, while the house rat originally comes from India. Hundreds of years ago, these rats began stowing away on ships as humans shipped goods and traveled around the world. These rats can survive in many kinds of environments. They had no trouble adjusting to life in unfamiliar countries as ships traveled from place to place. Both kinds of rats spread far and wide. Today they are common almost everywhere people live. Brown rats, for example, now live on every continent except Antarctica.

Wild species such as the Rajah spiny rat are found in many parts of Asia today.

Staying out of Sight

Rats generally prefer to live in places where they can stay hidden. Those in the wild often dig **burrows** in the ground. Some of these burrows are complex structures with many rooms and tunnels. Other rats create nests in hollow logs, under rocks, or in other hidden places. Some spend much of their time in trees. Rats living in urban areas often make their homes inside human-made structures. Basements, sewers, and other dark locations that people do not often visit are all common sites for rat nests.

Almost all rats are **nocturnal**. They stay hidden in their nests during the day and come out to search for food as the sun goes down. One of the few species that isn't nocturnal is the brown rat. It is active both at night and during the day.

Spaces in between rocks can make perfect hiding places for rats.

CHAPTER 2

Survival Skills

Like many other animals, rats spend much of their time and energy searching for food. Diets vary quite a bit among rat species. Some rats have a few favorite foods. Others will eat almost anything they can lay their paws on. Some species have diets that are mainly plant-based. For example, the Sulawesian white-tailed rat and Hoffman's rat eat primarily fruits and seeds. Other species prefer to hunt live prey. Some types of field rats prefer to eat tiny animals such as insects and slugs. Brown rats living in wild areas are more likely to hunt fish, birds, and even small **mammals** and lizards.

Brown and house rats in urban areas have learned to survive by eating a variety of human foods. They hide in alleyways behind restaurants to eat food that the businesses throw out. They also sneak into buildings to eat grains and other food that people are storing. Rats living near farms might feed on crops growing in fields.

Many city rats rely on trash as a source of food.

Sharp Senses

Rats rely on their powerful senses to track down food. Perhaps the most important of these senses is smell. As rats twitch their noses to sniff the air, they can pick up the scent of food from a great distance. They then follow the trail to reach the meal.

Sight is another sense that is important to rats. Because a rat's eyes are located on the sides of its head, it has a very wide range of vision. This helps a rat keep an eye out for threats.

A rat's large ears give it a strong sense of hearing. The ears' round, curved shape is perfect for picking up sound waves from the air.

Finally, touch plays a very important role in a rat's ability to sense its environment. Rats use their paws to feel vibrations in the ground as they walk. This tells them when other animals are nearby. Rats also have whiskers on the face that can help them feel for objects around them.

A rat's nose, whiskers, and paws all play a part in helping it navigate through its environment.

Lessons Learned

Rats are very intelligent animals. Their quick-thinking, problem-solving skills and long memories help them survive the many dangers they face both in the wild and in urban areas. For example, rats are very good at memorizing different paths they can take from place to place. They are also good at remembering locations where they are likely to find food. In addition, rats are good at figuring out shortcuts and alternate routes while on the move. This helps them avoid any dangers that might be in their way and keeps them from becoming lost.

Rats are good at learning new things and combining different pieces of information to solve problems. Scientists have trained rats to solve puzzles to reach food or avoid electric shocks. Once a rat learns how to solve a puzzle, it is usually able to remember the solution.

Rats can learn to make their way through complex mazes.

The Rat Race

Rats have no problem navigating around obstacles in their environment. Their strong legs and slender bodies make them very fast and **agile** on the ground. They have long claws on the ends of their toes and special pads on their rear feet. These features help them grip almost any kind of surface.

Many rat species are very good at climbing. Some of the strongest climbers, such as the Sulawesian white-tailed rat, spend most of their time in trees. Rats that do a lot of climbing usually have wider feet and longer tails than those that stay on the ground. Wide feet provide them with a better grip while climbing. A long tail helps the rats keep their balance while running across tree branches and other narrow paths.

Most rats are strong swimmers. They use this skill to capture fish and other **aquatic** prey. The ability to swim comes in handy for urban rats living in sewers. These rats might need to cross water to travel from place to place.

Rivers and streams are no obstacle for most kinds of rats.

A Dangerous World

Rats face many dangerous **predators**, whether they live in a wild forest or one of the world's busiest cities. Birds of prey, such as eagles, hawks, and owls, frequently hunt rats. These birds swoop down from above and snatch them with sharp claws. Large snakes and predatory lizards also eat rats in the wild. In urban areas, pet dogs and cats are common threats. Even other rats can be a danger. For example, brown rats have been known to prey on house rats.

One of a rat's best defenses from these enemies is to simply stay hidden. A rat's fur coloring often blends in well with the natural habitat. This helps the rat stay unseen as it darts around. Sometimes a rat is faced with a fight it can't escape by running away. Then it might try to intimidate its enemy by standing up tall on its rear legs and showing off its sharp teeth.

Barn owls are among the many bird species that prey on rats.

CHAPTER 3

Strength in Numbers

Rats are highly social animals. They tend to live together in large family groups. Within a family group, mother rats often share the same nesting area. Each rat has a distinct personality, and members of a family can tell each other apart by scent. Just like humans, rats form close bonds with their relatives. They wrestle and play with one another. They also help **groom** each other to keep clean. When it comes time to sleep, they cluster together to stay warm. These interactions are very important. Scientists have discovered that rats experience stress and depression if they cannot socialize.

Rats communicate with one another in many ways. In addition to touches and body language, they make many different sounds. Most of these sounds are so high-pitched that human ears cannot detect them. Rats also communicate using scents. For example, a rat leaves scent markings behind to warn rats that aren't part of its family group to stay away from its **territory**.

Rats love to climb and play with their family members.

Rapid Reproduction

Rats are famous for reproducing in large numbers very quickly. Members of a family group compete with one another to determine which ones **mate**. Rats try to show **dominance** by hissing, puffing up their fur, or standing up on their back legs. Only the biggest and strongest of them will mate.

Many rat species do not have a specific mating season. Instead, they mate and have babies all year long. Once a rat becomes pregnant, her babies are born in just three to four weeks. She is ready to mate again very soon afterward. As a result, a single rat might give birth to a **litter** of babies once every month, depending on the species. Each litter can have up to 22 babies, with the average litter containing 8 or 9 offspring. Young rats are ready to start mating and producing babies of their own when they are just 2 to 3 months old. This means a pair of rats can produce up to 15,000 **descendants** each year!

A rat might hiss and bare its teeth when trying to intimidate a rival.

Caring for Babies

Newborn rat babies are extremely tiny. For example, a newborn brown rat weighs just 0.18 ounces (5 grams). A baby rat is born without fur, so its entire body is covered in bare, bright-pink skin. Its toes are webbed, and it does not have any openings for its eyes. Instead, its eyeballs look like dark spots beneath its skin. Baby rats grow very quickly, though. At first, they spend all their time curled up in the family's nest where they drink milk from their mother. But by the time they are three to four weeks old, they look like smaller versions of adult rats. At this age, they are ready to stop drinking milk and start taking trips outside the nest.

Several females in a family group might have babies around the same time. This means there can be a lot of babies in a nest all at once. When this happens, the adult rats work together to care for the babies.

Mother rats care for their newborns by keeping them clean and feeding them.

CHAPTER 4

Rodent Relatives

Rats belong to a large group of animals called rodents. There are more than 2,000 different rodent species living today. They make up about half of all the world's mammal species. In addition to rats, rodents include such animals as squirrels, mice, beavers, and porcupines.

All rodents have sharp front teeth that never stop growing. In fact, rodents must constantly wear down their front teeth to keep them from growing too long. They do this by gnawing on objects or grinding their teeth against each other.

Some rodents can grow to be much larger than any rat species. The largest of all is the capybara. Capybaras can weigh up to 146 pounds (66 kilograms). Their bodies can measure as long as 4.4 feet (134 cm). The smallest rodent is the pygmy jerboa. This tiny animal is less than 2 inches (5 cm) long!

Unlike rats, capybaras do not have tails.

When "Rats" Aren't Really Rats

About two-thirds of all rodent species belong to the Muridae family. This family includes all rats, mice, and similar animals such as hamsters and gerbils. Like rats, other Muridae species are usually small animals with pointy faces and long bodies and tails.

All "true" rats belong to the *Rattus* genus. There are many Muridae species, however, that are outside of this genus but are mistakenly called rats. One example is the naked mole rat. This strange-looking animal has almost no fur covering its pink skin. It spends nearly all its time underground, rarely leaving its burrow.

Kangaroo rats are another group of rodents not considered true rats. In fact, they are not even part of the Muridae family. These animals are named for their large, powerful back legs that allow them to leap across long distances in a manner similar to a kangaroo.

The kangaroo rat spends a lot of time standing up on its strong rear legs.

CHAPTER 5

Living with Rats

Because rats often live among humans in towns and cities, they play many important roles in people's lives. In Southeast Asian countries such as Cambodia and Vietnam, rats are a common source of meat. People catch them by placing traps in rice or vegetable fields where the animals look for food.

In many parts of the world, rats are commonly kept as pets. Pet rats are also known as fancy rats. These are brown rats that have been **domesticated**. If handled with care, pet rats are very friendly. People can keep them in cages and feed them almost anything that humans eat. Many rat owners teach their pets to do tricks. Thanks to their intelligence, rats can learn how to do activities such as jump through hoops, play fetch, roll over, and run through obstacle courses. They can even learn their names and be trained to come when they are called, just as dogs can.

Domestic rats can be friendly, affectionate pets.

Lab Rats

Rats play a part in many scientific experiments. Because they don't take up much space and are easy to care for, scientists can keep large numbers of rats in their laboratories. In addition, the rat's ability to learn quickly makes it useful in a number of tests. For example, teaching rats to solve mazes has helped scientists discover how some animals think and learn new things. Attaching sensors to a rat's brain and having it perform various tasks has taught scientists which parts of the brain control different functions. Experiments with rats also help test new medications or types of surgery. They can even teach scientists new concepts about **genetics** and how diseases spread.

Many people believe that experimenting on rats is cruel. Rats are often harmed as part of these tests, and many of them die. Other people argue that the information such tests provide is very useful. Many scientists have changed their methods to be more humane, but animal testing remains a debated issue.

A laboratory might use dozens of rats for a single experiment.

Causing Trouble

As playful, intelligent, and helpful as rats can be, they can also cause problems. One issue is that they eat and damage a variety of human food sources. On farms, they feed on fruit, vegetable, and grain crops. They kill chickens and other small farm animals. In towns, they often find ways into food storage areas where there are large amounts of dried food. Not only do rats eat this food, they also leave behind droppings and urine, which ruin it.

Rats can help spread dangerous diseases, too. Rats themselves do not usually spread sickness directly to humans. They often carry fleas and lice in their fur, however, and these tiny creatures can pass along illnesses. One example of this is the plague, a disease spread through infected fleas. There have been a number of outbreaks of the plague around the world throughout history. Some of the worst were in the 1300s, when an estimated 50 million people died across Europe, Africa, and Asia.

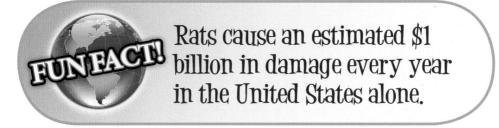

FUN FACT! Rats cause an estimated $1 billion in damage every year in the United States alone.

Rats can leave crops such as corn too damaged for humans to eat.

Finding a Balance

Rats are good at hiding, smart enough to avoid simple traps, and able to reproduce very quickly. As a result, it is very difficult to stop them from spreading or to decrease their numbers. Many cities hire workers to patrol streets and alleyways to catch rats. They also work to educate citizens about measures they can take to prevent rats from spreading into their homes. In 2015, the city of Chicago took a unique approach to rat control. Instead of trying to kill rats, it began placing rat food around the city. This is not regular food. It is tasty enough to attract rats and keep them coming back for more. However, it contains chemicals that make rats that eat it unable to reproduce.

It is unlikely that humans will solve their problems with rats anytime soon. But for all the trouble they cause, it is important to keep in mind that these amazing animals also do a lot of good.

A rat catcher in Mumbai, India, shows off the cages
he uses to collect rats from the city's streets.

Words to Know

agile (AH-jile) — able to move quickly and easily

aquatic (uh-KWAH-tik) — living or growing in water

burrows (BUR-ohz) — tunnels or holes in the ground made or used as a home by an animal

descendants (di-SEN-duhnts) — a person's or animal's offspring, their offspring, and so on into the future

domesticated (duh-MES-ti-kate-id) — tamed an animal so it can live with or be used by people

dominance (DAH-muh-nins) — influence or power

family (FAM-uh-lee) — a group of related plants or animals that is larger than a genus but smaller than an order

genetics (juh-NET-iks) — the study of how personal characteristics are passed from parents to children

genus (JEE-nuhs) — a group of related plants or animals that is larger than a species but smaller than a family

groom (GROOM) — to brush and clean

habitat (HAB-uh-tat) — a place where an animal or a plant is usually found

humane (hyoo-MANE) — kind and not cruel

litter (LIT-ur) — a number of baby animals that are born at the same time to the same mother

mammals (MAM-uhlz) — warm-blooded animals that have hair or fur and usually give birth to live young

mate (MAYT) — to join together to produce babies

nocturnal (nahk-TUR-nuhl) — active at night

predators (PRED-uh-turz) — animals that live by hunting other animals for food

prey (PRAY) — an animal that's hunted by another animal for food

species (SPEE-sheez) — one of the groups into which animals and plants of the same genus are divided; members of the same species can mate and have offspring

territory (TER-i-tor-ee) — an area of land claimed by a given individual or group

urban (UR-buhn) — having to do with or living in a city

Habitat Map

NORTH
AMERICA

SOUTH
AMERICA

PACIFIC

OCEAN

ATLANTIC

Rat Range

ARCTIC OCEAN

ASIA

EUROPE

AFRICA

PACIFIC OCEAN

OCEAN

INDIAN OCEAN

AUSTRALIA

Find Out More

Books

Armentrout, David. *The Facts on Rats*. Vero Beach, FL: Rourke, 2011.

Eagen, Rachel. *Rats Around Us*. New York: Crabtree Publishing Company, 2011.

Stefoff, Rebecca. *The Rodent Order*. New York: Marshall Cavendish Benchmark, 2009.

Visit this Scholastic Web site for more information on rats:
www.factsfornow.scholastic.com
Enter the keyword **Rats**

Index

Page numbers in *italics* indicate a photograph or map.

animal testing, 18, *36*, 37

babies, 26, *28*, 29
black rats. *See* house rats.
brown rats, 10, 13, 14, 22, 29, 34
burrows, 13, 33

capybaras, 30, *31*
claws, 21
climbing, 21, *24*
colors, 6, *8*, 9, 22, 29, 33
communication, 25, *27*
control, *40*, 41

damage, 38, *39*
defenses, 22, *27*
diseases, 38
dominance, 26, *27*

ears, 9, 17
eyes, 9, 17, 29

family groups, *24*, 25, 26, 29
fancy rats, 34
farms, 14, 38, *39*
females, 25, *28*, 29
fleas, 38
food, 6, 13, 14, *15*, 17, 18, 21, 29, 38
fur, *8*, 9, 22, 26, 29, 33, 38

grooming, 25, *28*

habitats, 6, *7*, 10, 14, 22
hiding, *12*, 13, 14, 22, 41
Hoffman's rats, 14
house rats, 10, 14, 22
hunting, 14, 21

intelligence, 18, *19*, 34, 37

kangaroo rats, *32*, 33

legs, 21, 22, 26, *32*, 33
lengths, 9, *9*, 30
lice, 38
litters, 26

mating, 26, 29
meat, 34
milk, 29
movement, 10, 18, *20*, 21, *24*, 33
Muridae family, 33

naked mole rats, 33
nests, 13, 25, 29
nocturnal activity, 13
Norway rats. *See* brown rats.
noses, *16*, 17

Osgood's rats, 9, *9*
owls, 22, *23*

(Index continued)

paws, *16*, 17, 21
people, 6, *7*, 10, 13, 14, *15*, 18, 34, *35*, *36*, 37, 38, *40*, 41
personalities, 25
pets, 22, 34, *35*
plague, 38
playing, *24*, 25, 34
predators, 17, 22, *23*, 34
prey, 14, 21, 38
pygmy jerboas, 30

Rajah spiny rats, *11*
Rattus genus, 33
rodents, 30, 33

scents, 17, 25
senses, *16*, 17
sizes, 9, *9*, 29, 30

socialization, 25
species, 9, 30, 33
speeds, 21
Sulawesian white-tailed rats, 9, *9*, 14, 21
swimming, *20*, 21

tails, 6, 9, 21, 33
teeth, 22, *27*, 30
territories, 25
toes, 21, 29
traps, 34, *40*

urban areas, 6, *7*, 10, 13, 14, *15*, 18, 21, 22, 34, *40*, 41

water, *20*, 21
weight, 29, 30
whiskers, *16*, 17

About the Author

Josh Gregory is the author of more than 90 books for kids. He has written about everything from animals to technology to history. A graduate of the University of Missouri–Columbia, he currently lives in Portland, Oregon.